Revelation Revisited

The Final Judgments

Volume 6

Revelation Revisited

The Final Judgments

Volume 6

DR. JEAN NORBERT AUGUSTIN

(BMM, MMM, DMM, DD, Th.D)

COPYRIGHT

© 2024 Dr. Jean Norbert Augustin

All Rights Reserved.

This book or any portion thereof may not be reproduced or used in any manner whatsoever without the express written permission of the publisher except for the use of brief quotations in a book review.

First printing 2024.

Publisher

NORBOOKS

Table of Contents

Revelation Revisited 1
    Volume 6 1
Revelation Revisited 2
    Volume 6 2
COPYRIGHT 3
ACKNOWLEDGMENTS 5
DEDICATION 6
EPIGRAPHS 7
PREFACE 1
CHAPTER 1 3
    THE BATTLE OF GOG AND MAGOG 3
CHAPTER 2 23
    THE FINAL JUDGMENTS 23
CHAPTER 3 41
    THE JUDGMENT SEAT OF CHRIST 41
CHAPTER 4 77
    DEATH DEMYSTIFIED 77
CHAPTER 5 126
THE GREAT WHITE THRONE JUDGMENT 126
CONCLUSION 149

ACKNOWLEDGMENTS

All my gratitude to the Holy Spirit for His continual and unwavering assistance.

DEDICATION

To all those who are looking for a deeper understanding of the very final events this world will witness.

EPIGRAPHS

"For we must all be revealed before the judgment seat of Christ; that each one may receive the things in the body, according to what he has done, whether good or bad." (2 Corinthians 5:10).

"I saw a great white throne, and him who sat on it, from whose face the earth and the heaven fled away. There was found no place for them." (Revelation 20:11-12).

Unless otherwise stated, all Scriptures quoted are from the World English Bible (WEB) by courtesy of Mr. Michael Paul Johnson, chief editor.

PREFACE

With this volume, our study of the Book of Revelation is nearing its end.

As in a classic tragedy, this volume is like the climax of the events – the moment when the drama reaches its culminating point.

As in a twenty-four day, this is the midnight hour. This is the moment when the darkness is at its zenith. One day is dying and a new day is about to dawn.

But before that new day dawns, a few things have to be set right. It's payback time. The party is over, the piper must be paid!

Indeed, the world may now seem to be a vast concert hall and life is the biggest party ever.

But, alas, every good thing has an end. Soon and very soon, the music will stop, the dancing will end, the disco lights will be turned off and all the revelers will have to part and go each their own way.

This is what Revelation Revisited Volume 6 will be all about.

CHAPTER 1

THE BATTLE OF GOG AND MAGOG

"And after the thousand years, Satan will be freed out of his prison,

and will come forth to deceive the nations which are in the four corners of the earth, Gog and Magog, to gather them together to the war; the number of whom is as the sand of the sea.

They went up over the breadth of the earth, and surrounded the camp of the saints, and the beloved city. Fire came down out of heaven, and devoured them."[1]

In Volume 5, we saw that Satan was chained and cast into the abyss for one thousand years. Thus, he couldn't do any harm during that period. Consequently, Jesus could establish His Millennial reign of peace on the earth.

This, of course, is not to mean that Jesus was afraid of Satan and needed to get him incarcerated before coming down to reign. The fact is that Jesus didn't want him to mar the beautiful and peaceful reign He was

---

[1] Revelation 20:7-9.

coming to set up. The Millennium was meant to reset the world to the stage where it stood before the Fall.

While the Millennium was meant to "wind" the world back to its original state for just one thousand years, the Kingdom that Christ will establish on earth when everything else will have been said and done will, indeed, last forever!

WHY SATAN IS RELEASED

In Volume 5, when we mentioned that Satan would be released after his one-thousand-year incarceration, we said that some would surely wonder why he should be.

Indeed, to our human mind, it would seem more logical to lock him in the abyss for good.

Imagine us setting a trap to catch a mouse that has been a nuisance in our house. The next morning, we check the trap and see that the trouble-maker has, indeed, been caught inside. And, for some absurd reason, we release the pest! Wouldn't that be unreasonable? Would our action not defeat all reason and logic?

Now, that would be only a little mouse dirtying the house, gnawing at our books, magazines, newspapers and textile!

But, in *Revelation*, it's not just a little mouse: it's Satan – the devil, the Serpent of Old, the arch-enemy! How much more he shouldn't be allowed out of the abyss?

Yet, *Revelation* tells us that he was released after the one thousand years.

But why?

During the Millennium, there will be two categories of saints who will reign with Christ: there will be those who will have experienced death and who will be raised to come and reign with Christ. Then there will be those who will still

be alive at His Coming - just as at the time of the Rapture:

"But we don't want you to be ignorant, brothers, concerning those who have fallen

asleep, so that you don't grieve like the rest, who have no hope.

For if we believe that Jesus died and rose again, even so those who have fallen asleep in Jesus will God bring with him.

For this we tell you by the word of the Lord, that we who are alive, who are left to the coming of the Lord, will in no way precede those who have fallen asleep.

For the Lord himself will descend from heaven with a shout, with the voice of the archangel, and with God's trumpet. The dead in Christ will rise first,

then we who are alive, who are left, will be caught up together with them in the clouds, to meet the Lord in the air. So we will be with the Lord forever.

Therefore comfort one another with these words[2].

Those who will not have experienced death at Christ's Coming - and who will not have been married then - will surely be able to do so during the Millennium. They will, thus, have children born to them. Those born during the Millennium will not have been exposed to Satan's evil influence. Consequently, they will not have been tempted by the devil to be tested. In other words, they will have had an easy life devoid of sin. Hence, they will have nothing to repent of. Moreover, they will have been *de facto* citizens under Christ's

---

[2] 1 Thessalonians 4:13-18.

rule – without having consciously confessed Him as their Saviour and Lord.

As salvation is only obtained by repentance and acceptance of Jesus as Saviour and Lord, they will have to go through the same procedure as anybody else.

That explains why Satan will have to be released after the Millennium. His mission, as it were, will not have been over yet. He will still have some devilish business to attend to:

"And after the thousand years, Satan will be freed out of his prison,

and will come forth to deceive the nations which are in the four corners of the earth, Gog and Magog, to gather them together to the war; the number of whom is as the sand of the sea."[3]

As the above Scriptures say, Satan will have to be released so that he may tempt and deceive those that have not yet accepted Jesus as Saviour and Lord. They will have to undergo the same test

as everybody else and be confronted with the alternatives of having to choose or reject Jesus, the only Way to the Father.

Another important "mission" on which he will have to go will be to gather all the impious nations from the four corners of the world to lead them into the final war against Christ and His people.

---

[3] Rev 20:7-8.

THE GOG AND MAGOG COUNTRIES

This mega-rebellion against God is referred to as Gog and Magog. In his book, the prophet Ezekiel mentioned that massive invasion of Israel by God's enemies:

"The word of Yahweh came to me, saying,

Son of man, set your face toward Gog, of the land of Magog, the prince of Rosh, Meshech, and Tubal, and prophesy against him,

and say, Thus says the Lord Yahweh: Behold, I am against you, Gog, prince of Rosh, Meshech, and Tubal:" [4]

---

[4] Ezekiel 38:1-3.

Chapters 38 and 39 of Ezekiel mention Gog and Magog and give some indication of the manner a massive invasion of Israel will take place at the end of this age.

Gog is the leader who will be at the head of a vast coalition of nations. He is said to be the *"prince of Rosh"* and to come from the land of Magog.

Forming part of that coalition, there will be Rosh – Gog's country -Meshech, Tubal, Persia. Tubal, Gomer, Togarmah, Meschech and Cush, among others.

Of these nine nations, only one is clearly identified: Persia, which is modern day Iran.

As for the eight others, there is no consensus although, in a general sense, the various interpretations point in some way or other towards the same regions.

This difficulty arises because the country names mentioned in Ezekiel 38 are ancient names. Overtime, the world geography has gone through great changes. Some blocks have split, some regions have been annexed as a result of populations' movement and conquests.

Moreover, certain nations have disappeared or have been assimilated with others.

Let's see what modern nations or countries have been associated with the eight ancient names.

Rosh and Magog are considered to be Russia and its satellites. Meschech and Tubal are deemed to be either Russia or Turkey. Cush is Sudan and Put is Libya. Gomer and Togarmah refer to Turkey.[5]

According to another source, Magog is Russia or part of it. Meschech and Tubal are a part of Turkey. Cush is Ethiopia. Put is Libya. Gomer is part of Turkey. Beth Togarmah is also a part of Turkey.[6]

---

[5] https://www.oxford bible church.co.uk. "The Identification of the Nations of Ezekiel 38. Accessed 11 April 2024.
[6] jashow.org

As we said above, the only country that's clearly named is Persia which, as we know, is modern day Iran. Should there be any doubt, we only have to look at the relationship between Iran and Israel. Iran has unequivocally declared its determination to erase Israel completely from the face of the earth! It's the number one priority on its agenda!

Except that the Iranian authorities don't know what lies in store for them:

---

https://jashow.org › Home › Prophecy: Who Are the Nations in Ezekiel 38? Accessed 11 April 2024.

"Then Yahweh will go out and fight against those nations, as when he fought in the day of battle.[7]

"This will be the plague with which Yahweh will strike all the peoples who have warred against Jerusalem: their flesh will consume away while they stand on their feet, and their eyes will consume away in their sockets, and their tongue will consume away in their mouth."[8]

It's interesting to see that those strange geographical names appear in Noah's genealogy[9]. Indeed, Genesis tells us that

---

[7] Zechariah 14:3.
[8] Zechariah 14:12.
[9] Genesis 10:1-6. 1 Chronicles 1:5.

Noah had three sons: Shem, Ham and Japheth.

Among the children of Japheth, were Gomer, Magog, Tubal and Meshech.

Gomer, in turn, begot Togarmah.

As for Ham, he fathered Cush and Put.

THE GOG-MAGOG REBELLION AND ITS END

God, in His Word, tells us how this massive rebellion will take place and what its outcome will be:

"They went up over the breadth of the earth, and surrounded the camp of the saints, and the beloved city. Fire came down out of heaven, and devoured them.

The devil who deceived them was thrown into the lake of fire and sulfur, where are also the beast and the false

prophet. They will be tormented day and night forever and ever." [10]

All those nations, mentioned n Ezekiel 38-39, will form a massive army that will march towards the holy city, Jerusalem and will congregate all around it with a view to completely annihilating it. As we have said above, there is already a nation that has this

---

[10] Revelation 20:9-10.

as its priority No. 1 on its agenda. That's Iran, referred to by its former name Persia in the Ezekiel's list!

Moreover, we saw, in a previous volume[11], that a way was prepared for that massive invasion of Jerusalem.

Indeed, during the Bowls of God's Wrath judgments, the third angel poured out his bowl on all rivers and springs. As a result of that, all their waters turned into blood.[12]

However, the Euphrates River received a quite different treatment. The sixth angel poured out his bowl on it and, lo, the River dried up! The apostle John tells us that that

---

[11] Revelation Revisited, Volume 4.
[12] Revelation 16:4.

happened so as to prepare a way *"for the kings that come from the sunrise"*[13] and *"for the war of the great day of God, the Almighty."*[14]

But, when that great invasion of Jerusalem will happen, God will send fire from Heaven, that will consume all of Israel's enemies in less than no time!

We quoted above a Scripture from Zechariah that speaks of what lies in store for the nations that will dare fight against Jerusalem!

The next event to occur will be the happiest one ever: the devil - who inspired all those nations to attack Jerusalem, and author of all

---

[13] Revelation 16:12.
[14] Revelation 16:14.

the evil that ever existed – will be thrown into the Lake of Fire. Thus, he will be reunited with his two acolytes, the Antichrist and the False Prophet who, by then, will already have been thrown there.[15] There, the three of them will burn and suffer for all eternity.

---

[15] Revelation 19:20.

CHAPTER 2

THE FINAL JUDGMENTS

After the devil has been cast into the Lake of Fire with his two accomplices, the next scene we are presented with is the Great White Throne.

It's time now for us to look at the question of Final Judgment.

In that regard, the question we should ask ourselves is the following: will believers and non-believers be judged together and at the same time? Will there be one judgment for both groups?

Many Christians are confused with regard to this question. But, when we study closely the Scriptures, we can have a better understanding of this subject.

TWO DIFFERENT JUDGMENTS

Before we go any further, let us straight away answer the questions put above.

The truth is that believers and non-believers will *not* be judged together. There will be two separate judgments – one for believers and one for non-believers. Neither will the bases and the consequences of the two judgments be the same! Isn't that rejoicing?

1: JUDGMENT AT THE HOUSE OF GOD

Let's back what we're saying with apt Scriptures.

"For the time [has come] for judgment to begin at the house of God. If it begins first at us, what will happen to those who don't obey the gospel of God?"[16]

---

[16] 1 Peter 4:17.

The apostle Peter tells us that judgment will begin at the house of God.

But what is the house of God?

Well, we know that, to all who accept Jesus as personal Saviour and Lord, He gives the power to become children of God.[17] Moreover, it is said that Jesus calls us His brothers – and sisters, of course:

"For both he who sanctifies and those who are sanctified are all from one, for which cause he is not ashamed to call them brothers,

---

[17] John 1:12.

saying, "I will declare your name to my brothers, In the midst of the congregation will I sing your praise."[18]

So, by believing in Jesus, we become members of God's family. In other words, we now constitute His household.

By saying that judgment will begin at the house of God, the apostle Peter is telling us that we, God's children, will be first to stand judgment.

I have sometimes heard preachers brandish this Scripture from 1 Peter 4:17 as a threat to believers. The implication of their threat is that believers should be careful because they

---

[18] Hebrews 2:11-12.

are in danger of being judged and, therefore, thrown into hell first!

Now, please, don't misunderstand me. Far from me to say that believers should take that Scripture lightly and completely disregard chastisement!

Instead, it must be taken with all the seriousness possible! Only, let's not go to the other extreme to cause an undue fright in God's children!

The apostle Peter is perfectly right in saying that judgment will start at the house of God.

A. The Sifting:

First, there will be a sifting as John the Baptist preached:

"His winnowing fork is in his hand, and he will thoroughly cleanse his threshing floor. He will gather his wheat into the barn, but the chaff he will burn up with unquenchable fire".[19]

Before Jesus comes again, He will cast out those who do not truly belong to Him. Remember the intruder at the wedding feast who didn't have his wedding dress on?[20]

Or, the five foolish Virgins who found the door shut and the Bridegroom already inside

---

[19] Matthew 3:12; Luke 3:17.
[20] Matthew 22:1-13.

while they were running around in the night looking for oil to buy for their lamps?[21]

B. The Apostasy:

Moreover, the Bible tells us that, before Jesus comes back, there will be a great apostasy.

*"Let no one deceive you in any way. For it will not be, unless **the departure** comes first, and the man of sin is revealed, the son of destruction"*.[22]

---

[21] Matthew 25:1-13.
[22] 2 Thessalonians 2:3, emphasis added.

This "departure" is translated *"apostasia"* in Greek and means "falling away".

"Apostasy" is thus defined:

"the repudiation of Christ and the central teachings of Christianity by someone who formerly was a Christian (Christ-follower)."[23]

In other words, "apostasy" is the rejection of religious and spiritual truths once received, believed and practiced.

---

[23] Wikipedia: "Apostasy in Christianity": Accessed 25 April 2024.

C. Love Grown Cold:

In the Olivet Discourse, Jesus gave a number of signs that will signal the end times and His Return. Among them, is the following:

"Because iniquity will be multiplied, the love of many will grow cold".[24]

One of the signs of the end times is the decrease in love. Indeed, among believers and non-believers alike, love has already begun to grow – maybe not cold yet, but lukewarm. Besides, the last of the Seven Churches of *Revelation* is Laodicea. And the

---
[24] Matthew 24:12.

main characteristic of that Church, that Jesus condemned was its lukewarmness.[25]

When the Church was founded in Acts 2, there was a spirit of love, compassion, empathy and unity among the believers. But, as the years elapsed, that love has considerably dwindled.

D. Faith Dwindled:

Not only love has diminished, faith, too, is no longer what it was in the Early Church. Foreseeing that, Jesus, once, asked the question:

---

[25] Revelation 3:14-22.

"Nevertheless, when the Son of Man comes, will he find faith on the earth?"[26]

That rhetorical question implies that Jesus was quite doubtful – if not skeptical - about the possibility of His finding faith on earth at His Return. Not that He didn't know. Being Divine, He is omniscient. But, by asking that reflexive question, He was giving His audience – and us – a hint and a warning so that we might watch over ourselves to keep our faith alive.

Based on what we've just seen, if faith will diminish, if love will dwindle and if there's

---

[26] Luke 18:8b.

going to be a great falling away, that will be the sifting John the Baptist prophesied. That will be a form of judgment that God will be exercising over His House.

In addition, the apostle John wrote the following:

"Little children, these are the end times, and as you heard that the Antichrist is coming, even now many antichrists have arisen. By this we know that it is the end times.

They went out from us, but they didn't belong to us; for if they had belonged to us, they would have continued with us. But they left, that they might be revealed that none of them belong to us." [27]

Thus, John also foresaw that, in the end times and with the imminence of the coming of the Antichrist, many would abandon the faith. Many, who once "believed" and "belonged" to the Church, will abandon the faith. For John, such "believers" were not really Christians – else, they would never have left!

Thus, Jesus will, exercise His judgment over God's House to make sure only those who persevere till the end will be saved.

---

[27] 1 John 2:18-19.

However, judgment beginning at the House of God has, yet, a more real and "tangible" meaning.

E. The Rapture:

Previous to the Great Tribulation, Jesus will come on the clouds to rapture His Church. We looked into that in detail in Volume 2.

By way of reminder, we'll quote the following Scriptures:

"But we don't want you to be ignorant, brothers, concerning those who have fallen

asleep, so that you don't grieve like the rest, who have no hope.

For if we believe that Jesus died and rose again, even so those who have fallen asleep in Jesus will God bring with him.

For this we tell you by the word of the Lord, that we who are alive, who are left to the coming of the Lord, will in no way precede those who have fallen asleep.

For the Lord himself will descend from heaven with a shout, with the voice of the archangel, and with God's trumpet. The dead in Christ will rise first,

then we who are alive, who are left, will be caught up together with them in the clouds, to meet the Lord in the air. So we will be with the Lord forever.

Therefore comfort one another with these words."[28]

The above Scriptures tell us that, one day, at the sound of God's trumpet and at the voice of the archangel, all dead believers will rise and, together with living believers, all with rise to meet Jesus in the air. That glorious event is called the Rapture – that is, the great Catching Up. All believers will, then, be united with Jesus forever.

---

[28] 1 Thessalonians 4:13-18.

When this happens, another judgment will take place. And that judgment will be the true judgment "at the house of God".

Let's now look into that.

CHAPTER 3

THE JUDGMENT SEAT OF CHRIST

"*Therefore also we make it our aim, whether at home or absent, to be well pleasing to him.*

**For we must all be revealed before the judgment seat of Christ; that each one may receive the things in the body, according to what he has done, whether good or bad.*"*[29]

"*But you, why do you judge your brother? Or you again, why do you despise your brother?*

---

[29] 2 Corinthians 5:9-10, emphasis added.

For we will all stand before the judgment seat of Christ."[30]

The Bible tells us that those who are in Christ have become a new creation:

"Therefore if anyone is in Christ, he is a new creation. The old things have passed away. Behold, they have become new."[31]

Sometimes we just quote this verse without really pondering its full meaning. However, if we do, we will understand that, if we are "in Christ", we have really become a new creation. The full meaning of that is that our nature has been completely changed: from sinners, we've become children of God; from

---

[30] Romans 14:10, emphasis added.

[31] 2 Corinthians 5:17.

being enemies of God, we've been reconciled to Him; from being carnal, we've become spiritual; from being corruptible, our bodies will become incorruptible; from being headed for hell, we're now heading for Heaven ...

In relation to our subject, our judgment also has changed – its timing, its place, its cause and its consequences.

Indeed, while unbelievers will appear before the Great White Throne, we, believers, will be judged at the Judgment Seat of Christ, as quoted above.

The Judgment Seat of Christ is known as the "*Bema*". In ancient Greece and Rome, races and games were often organized in amphitheaters. The winners then had to walk up a raised platform to receive their medals and other prizes. That raised platform was called a Bema.[32]

Do we know when this judgment will take place?

Well, as we saw above, it will happen *before* the judgment of non-believers. The Bible says that *"judgment will begin at the house of God"*.[33]

---

[32] Abundant Life: https://livingproof.co > what-is-the-bema-seat-of-christ. Accessed 20 May 2024.
[33] 1 Peter 4:17.

But it doesn't tell us in clear terms at what point in time this judgment will take place.

However, there are hints that can give us an idea of its timing.

*"Behold, I come **quickly**. My reward is with me, to repay to each man according to his work."*[34]

By "quickly", Jesus means that He is coming soon – that He won't delay. In other words, His arrival will precede the rest of the other end time events.

Also, the above Scripture tells us explicitly that He isn't coming empty-handed: He's coming with rewards!

---

[34] Revelation 22:12.

Already, there are a couple of things that should make us rejoice – at least, that should comfort us, believers.

Firstly, there is the fact that the Judge will be Jesus, our compassionate Saviour, and not the Father!

"For neither does the Father judge any man, but he has given all judgment to the Son"[35]

Not that the Father is not compassionate: He gave us Jesus out of love and compassion. But, we've seen His way of exercising judgment in the Old Testament! He sent thunder and lightning, and people were struck

---

[35] John 5:22.

dead! By comparison, Jesus will be a "milder" Judge.

The secondly good news is that Jesus is coming with rewards! And who doesn't like rewards?

Who are these rewards for? Are they for everybody"

That's what we shall examine now.

The apostle Paul has something very interesting and very eye-opening to say about that. Let's look at it:

"According to the grace of God which was given to me, as a wise master builder I laid a foundation, and another builds on it. But let each man be careful how he builds on it.

For no one can lay any other foundation than that which has been laid, which is Jesus Christ.

But if anyone builds on the foundation with gold, silver, costly stones, wood, hay, or stubble;

each man's work will be revealed. For the Day will declare it, because it is revealed in fire; and the fire itself will test what sort of work each man's work is.

If any man's work remains which he built on it, he will receive a reward.

If any man's work is burned, he will suffer loss, but he himself will be saved, but as through fire."[36]

---

[36] 1 Corinthians 3:10-15.

The above Scriptures are most important if we want to understand the judgment that believers will stand.

Six Building Materials:

Paul establishes a parallel between the Church and a house. The first thing he tells us in this metaphor is that he likens himself to a master builder. In the French version Louis Segond, this is translated as *"un sage architecte"* (a wise architect).

In that capacity, he laid the foundation. Indeed, Paul was an apostle – that is, somebody sent out to plant and pioneer churches. In other words, his calling was to lay the foundation of the Church in unexplored regions.

And who is that foundation? Paul tells us in unequivocal terms that it's Jesus Christ. Remember that Jesus, Himself, said: "I will build *my* Church"![37]

Moreover, Paul warns us that no-one can lay another foundation than Jesus Christ.

What the apostle says here is very important and – like it or not – eminently exclusive! In other words, outside of Jesus Christ, there is no other foundation – neither Buddha, nor Mohamed nor Krishna! That's why Jesus

---

[37] Matthew 16:18.

said: "*I am the way, the truth and the life and no-one goes to the Father except by me*".[38]

Next, Paul warns us about how we build upon that foundation. Some, he says, build in gold, some in silver, some in precious stones, some in wood, some in hay and some in stubble.

Whenever I teach on this subject, I like to take an example on housing estates in my country, Mauritius.

Before 1960, most houses were built with wood and iron sheets. Then, a number of cyclones hit the island – the most disastrous of all being cyclone Carol. Most of the houses

---

[38] John 14:6.

were utterly destroyed and victims had to live in refugee centres for some time.

Then, to re-lodge them, the government built a number of housing estates all over the island. All those houses were built on the same model – same type, same shape, same number of rooms, same colour, same look … To borrow a modern phrase, they were just "copy-paste" houses, as it were.

Those houses were rented to the cyclone victims for a minimal price over a number of years after which, they obtained their title deeds and became owners of their houses.

That was when things changed. Indeed, as long as the houses were leased, the occupants had no right to alter the structure of their houses.

But, once they had obtained full ownership of their houses, they made all kinds of alterations to them at the level of the size, shape, colour and every other aspect. Consequently, some of those houses have undergone such changes that they have become completely unrecognizable!

Yet, at the beginning, they all had received the exact same type and model of house! The "foundational" building was exactly the same for everybody. But then, each decided to build upon it differently.

But, to be frank, not all those houses look nicer now. Some planned well and had a reasonable sense of aesthetic. Consequently, their houses got a beautiful look on the inside and on the outside.

However, other houses became ugly, the alterations having been made haphazardly – no planning and no aesthetic! As a result, they've become real eye-sores!

In the spiritual sense, that is exactly what the apostle Paul says in the above Scriptures. Each and every true believer possesses the same and only "foundation", Jesus Christ. We all have believed in the same Jesus Christ, have received the same baptism, are indwelt with the same Holy Spirit, have the same Father and are heading towards the same Heaven.

But, our Christian walk is not the same for everybody. To clarify this, let's go back to Paul's metaphor.

He mentions six building materials: gold, silver, precious stones, wood, hay and stubble.

The first thing we notice is that these materials have been listed in descending order of importance and worth.

Also, they can be divided into two categories: three good ones – gold, silver and precious stones; three bad ones – wood, hay and stubble.

The reason I classify them as "good" ones and "bad" ones is that they will be tested by fire. It's obvious that gold, silver and precious stones stand fire much longer than wood, hay and stubble.

Diamond, for example, burns at 900 °C and melts at 4500 °C on condition that there is enough oxygen present to sustain ignition.[39] That's a tremendous temperature to attain and stand!

There is, yet, another distinction between these two sets of materials; while wood, hay and stubble grow *above* the ground, gold,

---

[39] Profound Physics "Can Diamonds Melt Or Burn (And How)? Accessed 28 April 2024.

silver and precious stones develop *below* the ground!

Let's now see what all this means.

Fire, in the Bible, is a symbol of judgment. For example, Sodom and Gomorrah were destroyed by fire. During his time-travel, the apostle John got a preview of the destruction of Babylon the Great by fire.[40]

But, with regard to the judgment at the Judgment Seat of Christ, fire is, rather, associated with the Holy Spirit. On the day of Pentecost, for example, the Holy Spirit descended upon the disciples in the form of tongues of fire.[41]

---

[40] Revelation 18:9; 18:18.
[41] Acts 2:1-4.

When John the Baptist preached to announce the coming of the Messiah, he said: *"I indeed baptize you with water, but he comes who is mightier than I, the latchet of whose sandals I am not worthy to loosen. He will baptize you in the Holy Spirit and fire"*.[42]

Moreover, the apostle Peter writes, in very clear terms, the following:

"Wherein you greatly rejoice, though now for a little while, if need be, you have been put to grief in various trials,

*that the proof of your faith, which is more precious than gold that perishes even though it is **tested by fire**, may be found to result in*

---

[42] Luke 3:16, emphasis added.

praise and glory and honor at the revelation of Jesus Christ".[43]

As we have said above, the trial at the Judgment Seat of Christ is for believers only.

But, are we, believers, not saved already? Why, then, will we have to appear at the Judgment Seat of Christ?

Indeed, do the Scriptures not say: "There is now, therefore, *no condemnation* for those who are in Christ"?[44]

Yes, the moment we believed and gave our hearts to Jesus, all our sins were blotted out by His blood. We now stand fully justified

---
[43] 1 Peter 1:6-7 emphasis added.
[44] Romans 8:1, emphasis added.

before God – not because of our own righteousness, but because of Christ's Righteousness imputed to us! Not because of what *we* did – but because of what *He* did! Salvation is a free gift from God in return for our faith:

"for all have sinned, and fall short of the glory of God;

being justified freely by his grace through the redemption that is in Christ Jesus".[45]

Why, then, will we have to appear at the *Bema*, the Judgment Seat of Christ?

---

[45] Romans 3:23-24.

The basis of this judgment – its rationale – can be found in the Epistle to the Ephesians.

"for by grace you have been saved through faith, and that not of yourselves; it is the gift of God,

not of works, that no one would boast.

For we are his workmanship, created in Christ Jesus for good works, which God prepared before that we would walk in them".[46]

Paul makes it clear that we are saved by grace through faith – and not by works. However, once saved, we must practise good works that God has prepared for us. It is of the utmost

---

[46] Ephesians 2:8-10.

importance that we understand that we are not saved *by* good works but *for* good works!

What do we mean by good works? Well, everything good – good character, good behaviour, good attitude, good words, good motives, and, most importantly, good actions. In short, service to God and service to Man.

Our good works are *not* forgotten:

"I heard the voice from heaven saying, "Write, 'Blessed are the dead who die in the Lord from now on.'" "Yes," says the Spirit, "that they may rest from their labors; for **their works follow with them**.*"*[47]

At the Judgment Seat of Christ, it's our post-salvation actions that will be judged. In 1

---

[47] Revelation 14:13, emphasis added.

Corinthians 3:10-15 that we quoted earlier in this chapter, Paul tells us that each believer's works will be tested by fire. And who, better than the Holy Spirit, can test our works?

"But as it is written, "Things which eye didn't see, and ear didn't hear, Which didn't enter into the heart of man, Whatever things God prepared for those who love him."

But to us, God revealed them through the Spirit. For the spirit searches all things, yes, the deep things of God.

For who among men knows the things of a man, except the spirit of the man, which is in him? Even so, no one knows the things of God, except God's Spirit".[48]

All our works after salvation are recorded by God. Of course, we don't mean that God has to act like a bookkeeper and write down everything we do. It's figurative language to enable us to get an idea of the proceedings so that we can better comprehend. God is omniscient – He even declares the end from the beginning.[49]

At the Judgment Seat of Christ, our works, as believers, will be tested by fire - in other words, the Holy Spirit will make an assessment of them.

---

[48] 1 Corinthians 2:9-11.
[49] Isaiah 46:9-10.

The good news is that this appraisal is not to determine our eternal destiny: that has already been dealt with and settled at Calvary!

On the contrary, this exercise will determine our reward. Remember that the Bema was, in Paul's days, a raised platform where athletes received their prizes.

It goes without saying that those who have built in gold will receive the best rewards available. The next best reward will go to those who built in silver. The third best reward will be awarded to those who built in precious stones.

We can make a parallel with the Olympic Games. Gold goes to the one who is ranked first, silver to the one who comes second, and bronze to the one ranked third.

The Miss World and Miss Universe pageants also follow the same pattern with the queen, the first princess and the second princess, in that order.

Those who built in gold, silver and precious stones will receive the best rewards because their works will stand and will pass the test by fire.

In other words, rewards will be proportionate to quality of works.

However, the comparison with the Olympic Games and Miss World or Miss Universe pageants ends here.

Indeed, on the podium of these human competitions, there are only three places.

Not so with the verdict at the Judgment Seat of Jesus!

Indeed, those who built with wood, hay and stubble will see their works burnt to ashes. But, the good news is that they *"will be saved, but as through fire"*.[50]

In other words, they will enter into eternity with Jesus, but without any reward.

I can't help remember the days when I taught high school. In our jargon, there was a phrase we used: "border line". This expression is used in the academic milieu to refer to cases

---

[50] 1 Corinthians 3:15.

where an examination candidate has obtained the bare minimum to obtain a pass.

Before the Judgment Seat of Jesus, we must not be content with passing the fire test by "border line"! Jesus didn't leave His Heavenly Throne, go through all that suffering and humiliation, shed all His blood for us so that we could get into Heaven *"as through fire"*! He wants us to get into Heaven, our heads lifted up high!

There is, yet, another important reason why we must get into Heaven with bright colours. Remember we said that Jesus is coming, but not empty-handed:

"Behold, I come quickly. My reward is with me, to repay to each man according to his work".[51]

"Watch yourselves, that we don't lose the things which we have accomplished, but that we receive a full reward"[52].

Among the rewards we'll receive, there will be crowns. The Bible mentions a number of them. We won't elaborate on that subject here so as not to drift from our subject. I have already done so in my Memoir titled: *"In Quest of Truth"*.[53]

---

[51] Revelation 22:12.
[52] 2 John 8.
[53] Jean Norbert Augustin: *"In Quest of Truth"*, ISBN-13: 979-8223735052. First published 22 April 2023.

With regard to crowns, Jesus gives us a word of warning:

"I come quickly. Hold firmly that which you have, so that no one takes your crown."[54]

This implies that there's already a crown reserved for us. And Jesus wishes very strongly that we hold on to it!

How, then, can we take Jesus's promises lightly and enter eternity *"as through fire"*?

Our crown will bear testimony to the perfect work Jesus accomplished on the Cross. Additionally, it will be a testimony to our

---

[54] Revelation 3:11.

good actions performed as faithful and obedient believers.

But there is, yet, another major reason why we must strive to get our crown and make sure no-one takes it from us.

The one who could take it away from us is, of course, the devil. However, we may also give it away or barter it – pretty much as Esau who sold his birthright to his younger brother Jacob for a mere bowl of pottage![55]

There are a number of circumstances in which believers could surrender their crown. But to go lengthily into that would draw us away from our main theme.

---

[55] Genesis 25:29-34.

Let's, rather, see why it is of the utmost importance that we get our crown and keep it safe until we meet with Jesus in eternity.

"When the living creatures give glory, honor, and thanks to him who sits on the throne, to him who lives forever and ever,

the twenty-four elders fall down before him who sits on the throne, and worship him who lives forever and ever, and will throw their crowns before the throne, saying,

"Worthy are you, our Lord and our God, to receive the glory, the honor, and the power, for you created all things, and because of your desire they existed, and were created."[56]

---

[56] Revelation 4:9-11.

One day, we shall be united with Jesus and spend eternity praising and worshipping Him. The above Scriptures relate a preview of that such as the apostle John witnessed during the revelation he received.

As we see above, the twenty-four elders around the Throne cast their crowns before the Throne as they worship.

Some commentators believe that those twenty-four elders represent a picture of the Church in Heaven.

Anyway, John describes another scene in Heaven that explicitly shows us a preview of believers in Heaven:

"After these things I saw, and behold, a great multitude, which no man could number, out

of every nation and of all tribes, peoples, and languages, standing before the throne and before the Lamb, dressed in white robes, with palm branches in their hands.

They cried with a loud voice, saying, "Salvation be to our God, who sits on the throne, and to the Lamb."

All the angels were standing around the throne, the elders, and the four living creatures; and they fell before the throne on their faces, and worshiped God,

saying, "Amen! Blessing, glory, wisdom, thanksgiving, honor, power, and might, be to our God forever and ever! Amen."

One of the elders answered, saying to me, "These who are arrayed in white robes, who are they, and where did they come from?"

I told him, "My lord, you know." He said to me, "These are those who came out of the great oppression. They washed their robes, and made them white in the Lamb's blood."[57]

God loves everybody – irrespective of race, nation, tribe, colour, tongue and so on. That's why He sent Jesus to save all mankind.

During John's time-travel, Jesus allowed him to have a preview of a cosmopolite crowd around God's Throne in Heaven.

---

[57] Revelation 7:9-14.

And what are they doing?

Worshipping!

Similarly, this is going to be the believers' main activity in Heaven! That's why it's of the utmost importance that we get our crown and not allow anybody to take it from us. We need it to cast it at Jesus's feet before the Throne for He, alone, deserves all praise and glory!

CHAPTER 4

DEATH DEMYSTIFIED

Death is a mystery. It's something that's unavoidable. It's every single human being's lot. We are all born to die. Paradox of paradoxes! The very idea of death sparks fright in the human mind.

Yet, we know very little about it.

Or, don't we?

Yet, the concept was first introduced in Genesis, the book of the beginnings.

As we know, God warned Adam and Eve that, the day they would eat of the tree of the knowledge of good and evil, they would die.

"Yahweh God commanded the man, saying, "Of every tree of the garden you may freely eat:

but of the tree of the knowledge of good and evil, you shall not eat of it: for in the day that you eat of it you will surely die."[58]

Indeed, the Bible lifts up the veil over death and helps us understand what it is.

---

[58] Genesis 2:16-17.

Under the Old Covenant, the soul of every dead human being went to a place called "*Sheol*" in Hebrew. The New Testament being written in Greek, that place is called "*Hades*".

Let's look at a few Old Testament references to *Sheol*.

Believing the lie that his dear son Joseph had been devoured by a wild animal, Jacob said:

"*For I will **go down** to Sheol to my son mourning.*"[59]

---

[59] Genesis 37:35, emphasis added.

Speaking of his last son Benjamin, again Jacob said:

"*My son shall not **go down** with you; for his brother is dead, and he only is left. If harm befall him by the way in which you go, then you will **bring down** my gray hairs with sorrow to Sheol.*"[60]

"*Yahweh kills, and makes alive: He **brings down** to Sheol, and brings up*".[61]

As he had grown old, David gave instructions to his son Solomon with regard to Joab who had been guilty of shedding much blood.

---

[60] Genesis 42:38, emphasis added.
[61] 1 Samuel 2:6.

*"Do therefore according to your wisdom, and don't let his gray head **go down** to Sheol in peace."*[62]

In the book of *Job*, there is much allusion to Sheol. Here, Job is explaining how the wicked prosper in all spheres of their lives until the inexorable end comes:

*"They spend their days in prosperity. In an instant they **go down to Sheol**."*[63]

During a time when David was facing rebellion on the part of his son Absalom, he also experienced betrayal by a close unnamed friend. Seeing violence all around, he pleads

---
[62] 1 Kings 2:6.
[63] Job 21:13, emphasis added.

to God: *"Let death come suddenly on them. Let them **go down** alive into Sheol."*[64]

In the powerfully anointed message the apostle Peter preached on the day of Pentecost, he quoted David who was speaking prophetically about Jesus. Notice how *"Sheol"* is now referred to as *"Hades"*.

"Because you will not leave my soul in Hades, Neither will you allow your Holy One to see decay."[65]

The Scriptures we've quoted above give us something strange but revelatory to

---

[64] Psalm 55:15, emphasis added.
[65] Acts 2:27.

understand. Indeed, we notice that everybody went to *Sheol* – the good and the wicked!

You would be shocked if we told you something: even Jesus went to *Sheol* when He died!

How do we know?

Well, the verse of Acts 2:27 quoted above speaks of "the Holy One" in capitalized initial letters.

It's obvious that this appellation cannot apply to David! In fact – as is often the case in *Psalms* – David was speaking prophetically about Jesus. The phrase "the Holy One" clearly refers to Jesus.

Indeed, the Scripture of Acts 2:27 speaks of Jesus who went to Hades and whose body did not decay for He rose from the dead exactly as He had prophesied.

It's important to make it clear here that "Hades" is not Hell as some consider the latter to be the place where the lost will go to spend eternity! Hades is not the eternal Lake of Fire!

The apostle Paul also gives us an indication that Jesus, too, went to Hades after His death:

"Therefore he says, "When he [Jesus] *ascended on high, he led captivity captive, and gave gifts to men."*

Now this, "He ascended," what is it but that he also first descended into the lower parts of the earth?

He who descended is the same also who ascended far above all the heavens, that he might fill all things."[66]

The emphasized verse tells us very clearly that Jesus definitely *"descended into the lower parts of the earth"* – which must be Hades!

Do we have any indication where Hades is located?

---

[66] Ephesians 4:8-10, emphasis added.

We can't tell with certainty. But, notice how most references to Sheol or Hades are accompanied implicitly by the preposition "*down*" and explicitly by the verb "*descend*" – which implies a *downward* movement.

In the Ephesian Scripture quoted above, it is more clearly said that Jesus "*descended into the lower parts of the earth*".

It must, therefore, be a space, buried deep down in the belly of the earth. Because it is a place where the souls of dead people are confined, it must be a spiritual place which cannot be found by human means.

Why did Jesus have to go down to *Sheol*?

Let's try to answer this question with apt Scriptures.

"Because Christ also suffered for sins once, the righteous for the unrighteous, that he might bring you to God; being put to death in the flesh, but made alive in the spirit;

*in which he also went and preached to the spirits **in prison**".*[67]

What can that "prison" where Jesus went to preach "in the spirit" be?

If He was in the spirit, it's clear that He was dead. Where, then, could He have gone?

The obvious answer must be to Hades!

We remember that, when Jesus was crucified, there was a brigand crucified on either side of

---

[67] 1 Peter 3:17-18.

him. One of them was cursing and provoking Jesus.

The other, on the other hand, turned to Jesus with a contrite heart and said:

"Lord, remember me when you come into your kingdom".[68]

"Assuredly I tell you, today you will be with me in Paradise."[69]

The above verse clearly states that Jesus and the repentant brigand would go to Paradise *that same day.*

---

[68] Luke 23:42.
[69] Luke 23:43.

But did Jesus not rise from the dead? Did He not appear to His disciples for forty days before ascending to Heaven?[70]

How, then, could He be with the brigand in Paradise?

As Jesus could not have lied, He must, indeed, have been in Paradise with the brigand during the three days His body was in the tomb, then risen from the dead before ascending to Heaven forty days later!

But this raises another question: did Jesus, the just and the wicked all go to the same place, Hades?

---

[70] Acts 1:4-9.

In the Lukan gospel, Jesus, Himself, gives us a very clear answer through a highly graphic anecdote.

"Now there was a certain rich man, and he was clothed in purple and fine linen, living in luxury every day.

A certain beggar, named Lazarus, was laid at his gate, full of sores, and desiring to be fed with the crumbs that fell from the rich man's table. Yes, even the dogs came and licked his sores.

It happened that the beggar died, and that he was carried away by the angels to Abraham's bosom. The rich man also died, and was buried.

In Hades, he lifted up his eyes, being in torment, and saw Abraham far off, and Lazarus at his bosom.

He cried and said, 'Father Abraham, have mercy on me, and send Lazarus, that he may dip the tip of his finger in water, and cool my tongue! For I am in anguish in this flame.'

"But Abraham said, 'Son, remember that you, in your lifetime, received your good things, and Lazarus, in like manner, bad things. But now here he is comforted and you are in anguish.

Besides all this, between us and you there is a great gulf fixed, that those who want to pass from here to you are not able, and that none may cross over from there to us.'

"He said, 'I ask you therefore, father, that you would send him to my father's house;

for I have five brothers, that he may testify to them, lest they also come into this place of torment.'

"But Abraham said to him, 'They have Moses and the prophets. Let them listen to them.'

"He said, 'No, father Abraham, but if one goes to them from the dead, they will repent.'

"He said to him, 'If they don't listen to Moses and the prophets, neither will they be persuaded if one rises from the dead'"[71].

This gospel narrative is very important in so far as it is the only passage that gives us such

---

[71] Luke 16:19-31.

a clear idea of the after-life. Its importance is further enhanced by the fact that the narrator is no less a person than Jesus, Himself!

Many consider that this passage is a parable. But the Bible doesn't explicitly say that it is a parable. Most often - though not always - there is, in the Bible, a subtitle that signals a parable. And sometimes the gospel author, himself, states clearly, at the beginning of a narration, that what follows is a parable. A very good example is Matthew 13 which is, so to say, all parables!

But such is not the case here.

More importantly, parables do not typically mention names. However, this narrative *does* mention the name Lazarus, one of the characters.

Moreover, parables are stories that are meant to be read and understood on two levels – natural and spiritual. They are like musical scores written on two different scales.

But the narrative we have quoted above is quite plain and straightforward. It has no undertone appended to it.

This narrative presents us with two diametrically different characters.

On one hand, we see a very rich man, dressed in costly clothing and feasting daily.

On the other hand, we see an extremely poor man, Lazarus, whose body is covered with sores. The expression *"was laid at his* [the rich man's] *gate"*, being in the passive, implies that he didn't lie there unassisted, but that somebody – people – laid him there. In other words, he must have been a miserably helpless creature!

There, famished, he lay, waiting for some crumbs from the rich man's table to be thrown to him. But none ever came his way!

Heartless, the rich man kept feasting and making merry without even once throwing something to Lazarus.

The story says *"even* the dogs came to lick his sores". The word *"even"* emphasizes the contrast between the rich man and the dogs.

As opposed to the rich man, the dogs came to lick his sores.

But why would they do that?

Dogs lick their wounds because their saliva contain certain antibacterial substances. They use their tongue to clean up the wound and their saliva helps the healing process. Their saliva is said to be their "first-aid kit".[72]

In a sense, the dogs proved to be more human than the rich man!

What interests us in this narrative with regard to our study is what happened next.

---

[72] https://richmondvalleyvet.com: "Dog saliva facts that you probably didn't know about". 14 February 2018. Posted by Kiran. Accessed: 05 May 2024.

In the course of time, they both die. The poor man is carried by angels into what the Bible calls Abraham's bosom. Some call it Paradise.

As for the old man, once buried, he opens his eyes and finds himself in a place of torment while, afar off, he sees Lazarus peacefully resting in Abraham's bosom!

A prey to unbearable suffering, he pleads to Abraham to send Lazarus over to him in order to dip the tip of his finger in water to cool his tongue!

But, no matter how intensely he begs, he receives no help for, as Abraham has told him, they are separated by a gulf so vast it cannot be crossed!

Of course, I'm not going to exploit this passage extensively. That would take us away from our subject – Hades!

Before we move on with our study, allow us to make something clear.

Indeed, the reason why the rich man was sent to a place of torment was not his wealth. God saves the rich as much as He saves the poor.

However, his fate must have been due to absence of concern for his soul's nourishment: he contented himself with feeding his body only. Basking in his extravagant wealth and luxury, he may never have had the least thought of the after-life.

More pragmatically, his heartlessness and absence of concern for the famished beggar lying at his gate made of him an apt candidate to the place of eternal torment!

Getting back to our subject, we see in this narrative a very revelatory detail: both, the rich man and Lazarus found themselves in the same vast space, but separated by an impassable gulf!

This justifies what we said above – namely that all dead souls went into Hades, the just and the unjust. But they were segregated!

The obvious conclusion we can draw is that Hades is *one vast* space with *two* compartments and a *partition* in between.

The just went to the "good" compartment, Abraham's bosom or Paradise; the wicked went to the "bad" compartment, the place of torment.

That having been said, we think it would be safe to say that Jesus and the repentant brigand went to the "good" compartment of Hades for Jesus explicitly mentioned the word "Paradise" in His response to the repentant brigand crucified beside Him.

But, what must have happened during those three days Jesus was in the tomb? Can we gather some hint with regard to this from the Scriptures? Did He rest, as some believe? That's not the like of Jesus!

Remember how, during His earthly ministry, He was indefatigable:

"The foxes have holes, and the birds of the sky have nests, but the Son of Man has no place to lay his head."[73]

To answer the question asked above as to what must have happened during the three days that Jesus spent in the tomb, we may perhaps find an indication in a verse we quoted above:

"Because Christ also suffered for sins once, the righteous for the unrighteous, that he might bring you to God; being put to death in the flesh, **but made alive in the spirit;**

---

[73] Luke 9:58.

in which he also went and preached to the spirits in prison".[74]

Peter, under the inspiration of the Holy Spirit, informs us that the "dead" Jesus went to preach to the spirits in prison.

What was that "prison"?
Since it was inhabited by spirits, it must have been the "good" compartment of Hades, Paradise where the just went.

From the above, we also learn that, far from resting, Jesus preached to those in Paradise. What a revelation! Indefatigable, as we said!

Peter confirms that in yet another Scripture:

---
[74] 1 Peter 3:17-18, emphasis added.

"Forasmuch then as Christ suffered for us in the flesh, arm yourselves also with the same mind; for he who has suffered in the flesh has ceased from sin;

that you no longer should live the rest of your time in the flesh to the lusts of men, but to the will of God.

For we have spent enough of our past time living in doing the desire of the Gentiles, and to have walked in lasciviousness, lusts, drunken binges, orgies, carousings, and abominable idolatries.

They think it is strange that you don't run with them into the same excess of riot, blaspheming:

who will give account to him who is ready to judge the living and the dead.

For to this end was **the gospel preached even to the dead**, *that they might be judged indeed as men in the flesh, but live as to God in the spirit."*[75]

To summarize what Peter says, we, believers, have, in the past, spent enough time living in sin. Now, it's time we start seriously living a life that glorifies Christ. Those who are not in Christ will find it strange that we no longer live the way they do.

But the fact is that all will, one day, have to give an account to Christ who will come to

---

[75] 1 Peter 4:1-6, emphasis added.

judge the living and the dead. That's why Jesus went to preach to the dead in Hades for – though we're in the flesh on earth, we're expected to live in the spirit the way God wills.

Now that we've established the fact that Jesus did preach to the dead in Paradise, a few questions may arise in our mind: "What did He preach?" Was He giving the dead a second chance to be saved? Did He preach to the wicked also?

The Bible provides no answer to these questions.

But one thing is clear: He didn't preach to the wicked for He went only to Paradise, the place reserved for the just!

Was He giving the dead a second chance to get saved? Logically not, for the dead in Paradise were already just – they were people like Jacob, Isaac, Samuel, David, John the Baptist and so on.

Besides, the Bible says: *"Inasmuch as it is appointed for men to die once, and after this, judgment,"*.[76]

A 1967 James Bond movie was titled *"You Only Live Twice"*; but the Bible declares that we die only once, after which comes judgment.

So there is no second chance: just judgment!

---

[76] Hebrews 9:27.

When Jesus went to preach to the deceased in Paradise, it must have been essentially to tell them what He said on the Cross: *"It is finished!"*[77] In other words, to inform them of the fact that His blood had already been shed – that His vicarious death had accomplished what was epitomized by the Old Testament animal sacrifices. In short, that full and perfect atonement had been accomplished.

Hades is, however, not the permanent and definitive abode of the dead. They were sent there in the interim, pending their being sent to their definitive location – very much the same way a person under arrest is first locked in police custody until he is officially judged

---

[77] John 19:30.

and condemned. Then is he sent to jail to serve time!

The author of the Epistle to the Hebrews tells us something very important:

"According to the law, nearly everything is cleansed with blood, and apart from shedding of blood there is no remission."[78]

In Old Testament days, animal's blood was used to temporarily cover sins – to offer propitiation. It was a type of the holy blood Jesus, the Lamb of God, was coming to shed later on – not just to cover sins but to wash them away for good!

---

[78] Hebrews 9:22.

After death, the just were sent to Paradise pending the shedding of Jesus's blood. When Jesus died and went to Paradise, that was the "*gospel* [good news] *he went to went to preach to those in prison*".[79]

When Jesus delivered His inaugural message in the synagogue in Nazareth, among other things, He declared He had been sent to set the captives free.[80]

Usually, when we preach, we take that to mean that Jesus had come to free people from sins, passions, vices and addictions. That's true in the short term – with regard to our temporal existence.

---

[79] 1 Peter 3:19.
[80] See Luke 4:18-19.

But, the Lord's declaration went much further than that. He had, more importantly, been sent to set free the just who were temporarily kept in the "prison" called Paradise.

Now that we've satisfactorily established the fact that Jesus went to Hades after His death to preach to those "imprisoned" there, let's see if we can have an idea of what happened next.

Is there a way to know? When Peter preached on the day of Pentecost, three thousand souls were added to the Church.[81]

---

[81] Acts 2:41.

When Peter and John preached in Jerusalem, they *"filled* [Jerusalem] *with* [their] *teaching"*.[82]

Even when we, modern-day ministers preach, things do happen – albeit not as dramatic!

Could it be that Jesus took the pain to descend to *"the lower parts of the earth"* to preach to dead souls and nothing happened?

Could it be that the apostles' preaching – and ours – proved to be more powerful and more productive than Jesus's? Eminently doubtful!

When Jesus breathed His last on the Cross, a number of supernatural phenomena took

---

[82] Acts 5:28.

place. Just before, complete darkness had fallen upon the earth, lasting for three hours! Then *"Behold, the veil of the temple was torn in two from the top to the bottom. The earth quaked and the rocks were split.*

The tombs were opened, and many bodies of the saints who had fallen asleep were raised;

and coming forth out of the tombs after his resurrection, they entered into the holy city and appeared to many."[83]

At the moment Jesus died, dead bodies were brought back to life. However, they walked into Jerusalem to be seen by many *only after* His resurrection. It couldn't have been *before*

---

[83] Matthew 27:51-53, emphasis added.

because Jesus had to be the first fruit of all those ever to be resurrected!

Of course, there had been many previous cases of people raised from the dead before Jesus – such as the well-known example of Lazarus[84] and that of the son of the widow of Nain,[85] both raised by Jesus, Himself.

In the Old Testament, the prophet Elijah raised the son of the widow of Zarephath.[86] Elisha later on raised the Shunammite widow's son.[87]

---

[84] John 11:1-45.
[85] Luke 7:11-17.
[86] 1 Kings 17:17-24.
[87] 2 Kings 4:18-37.

Spectacular as those resurrections had been, the "beneficiaries" all eventually died for good.

But not so for Jesus and the resurrected saints! Notice that Matthew said that the dead who came back to life at Jesus's resurrection *appeared only* to many – which implies that they didn't go back to live on on earth, but then vanished from their sight!

If that was so, where did they go after having appeared to many?

The Scriptures may well have something to tell us regarding this matter:

"Therefore he says, "When he [Jesus] *ascended on high, he led* **captivity captive,** *and gave gifts to men".*[88]

"You have ascended on high. ***You have led away captives.*** *You have received gifts among men, Yes, among the rebellious also, that Yah God might dwell there."*[89]

Both, Paul and David, speak of Jesus ascending to Heaven, leading *"captivity captive"*.

As we saw above, Jesus went to *Sheol* - or *Hades* - and preached to those "imprisoned" there. The expression "led captivity captive" may well mean that Jesus set them free –

---

[88] Ephesians 4:8, emphasis added.
[89] Psalm 68:18, emphasis added.

hence, the apparition of some of them in Jerusalem - and ascended to Heaven with them.

The way the psalmist puts it – especially with the contiguity of two independent clauses and the use of the plural – makes it even more plausible:

*"You have ascended on high. You have led away **captives**"*.

The captives He set free and took to Heaven with Him may have served as a trophy to exhibit His victory over death and Hades:

"When I saw him, I fell at his feet like a dead man. He laid his right hand on me, saying, "Don't be afraid. I am the first and the last, and the Living one. **I was dead, and behold, I am alive forevermore. I have the keys of Death and of Hades.**"[90]

The apostle Paul also, on a taunting and defying tone, celebrates Jesus's triumph over death and Sheol:

"Death is swallowed up in victory."

"Death, where is your sting? Hades, where is your victory?"[91]

---

[90] Revelation 1:17-18, emphasis added.
[91] 1 Corinthians 15:54-55.

Remember we said that Sheol was divided into two compartments – one for the just and one for the wicked.

The "good" section was called Abraham's Bosom or Paradise. That's where Jesus went to preach during the three days His body lay in the tomb.

When He rose from the dead, He apparently took the souls of the just with Him to Heaven.

Consequently, Abraham's Bosom or Paradise has been vacated and is now empty.

Let's look at a few Scriptures to justify that.

"Being therefore always of good courage, and knowing that, **while we are at home in the body, we are absent from the Lord***;*

for we walk by faith, not by sight.

We are of good courage, I say, and are willing rather to be absent from the body, and to be at home with the Lord."[92]

Paul is here saying two important things: Firstly, as long as we are in the body, we are away from the Lord. Secondly, it is preferable to be out of the body and be *at home* with the Lord.

Notice that Paul uses the phrase "*at home*" to signify to be in the Lord's presence. Indeed,

---

[92] 2 Corinthians 5:6-8, emphasis added.

Christian believers' true and definitive home is Heaven. We are merely pilgrims on this earth!

This reminds us of the famous hymn "This World Is Not My Home":

"This world is not my home, I'm just a-passing through,
My treasures are laid up somewhere beyond the blue;
The angels beckon me from heaven's open door,
And I can't feel at home in this world anymore."[93]

---

[93] Hymnary.Org: Arranger: Albert E. Brumley. Copyright: 7, Ren. 1965 Albert E. Brumley & Sons Accessed: 10 May 2024.

In his Letter to the Philippians, Paul makes it crystal clear that, as Christians, our true citizenship is not here on earth:

*"**For our citizenship is in heaven**, from where we also wait for a Savior, the Lord, Jesus Christ;*

who will change the body of our humiliation to be conformed to the body of his glory, according to the working whereby he is able even to subject all things to himself."[94]

Paul makes things even much clearer in the following Scriptures:

"For to me to live is Christ, and to die is gain.

---

[94] Philippians 3:20-21, emphasis added.

But if to live in the flesh, this will bring fruit from my work; then I don't make known what I will choose.

But I am in a dilemma between the two, having the desire to depart and be with Christ, which is far better.

Yet, to remain in the flesh is more needful for your sake."[95]

In the Scriptures quoted above, Paul expresses a number of very important facts.

First of all, he says that, for the believer, to die is gain. This sounds very much like a paradox. While people generally fear death,

---

[95] Philippians 1:21-24.

how come he says that death is an advantage to us? Death is beneficial? How queer!

But Paul explains himself.

He says he's in a fix. He doesn't know which is better – to live or to die?

If he dies, he'll, at once, be with Jesus. And that's, by far, much better than to live.

However, if he stays, he'll be able to continue preaching, teaching and making disciples.

In the former case, he'll be the one benefiting; in the latter, his disciples will gain.

Beyond Paul's dilemma, what interests us in this argument is what he says about death:

death will transport him immediately into Jesus's presence!

This and his statement that death is gain confirm what we said above – namely that Abraham's Bosom is now empty for, once Jesus has made atonement for our sins, believers, at death, go directly into the presence of the Lord! However, unbelievers still go to the bad compartment of Sheol, as we are going to see as we proceed.

No wonder, the Bible says: *"Therefore if anyone is in Christ, he is a new creation. The old things have passed away. Behold, they have become new."*[96]

---

[96] 2 Corinthians 5:17.

This newness goes much further than what we usually think. From walking in the flesh, we start walking in the spirit; from being headed for hell, we start on our way to Heaven; from being judged at the Great White Throne, we are judged at the Judgment Seat of Christ; from being judged to be punished, we are judged to be rewarded; from going to Sheol, we go into the Lord's presence! Hallelujah!

CHAPTER 5

THE GREAT WHITE THRONE JUDGMENT

The spectacle that presents itself to John now is really awesome and frightening.

"I saw a great white throne, and him who sat on it, from whose face the earth and the heaven fled away. There was found no place for them.

I saw the dead, the great and the small, standing before the throne. Books were opened. **Another book was opened, which is the book of life**. *The dead were judged out of* *the things which were written in the books, according to their works.*

The sea gave up the dead who were in it. Death and Hades gave up the dead who were in them. They were judged, each one according to his works.

Death and Hades were thrown into the lake of fire. This is the second death, the lake of fire.

If anyone was not found written in the book of life, he was cast into the lake of fire."[97]

Many believers have mistakenly thought that this is where we will, one day, stand judgment. But we have amply shown that we,

---

[97] Revelation 20:11-15, emphasis added.

believers, will be judged at the *Bema* – the Judgment Seat of Jesus. Besides, the outcome won't be condemnation in hell, but rewards based on the quality of our works after salvation.

The spectacle that offers itself to John before the Great White Throne is astounding and spine-chilling.

Indeed, the apostle sees all the dead standing before the Throne – all kinds of dead people raised back to life: the great and the small, the rich and the poor, the Blacks and the Whites, Communists and Capitalists, masters and slaves, monarchs and subjects, and so on.

John sees Someone sitting on the Great White Throne.

Who can that One be?

It can be no-one else but Jesus!

How do we know?

Well, the Bible tells us that the Father judges no-one: He's given all judgment to His Son Jesus.[98]

His presence on the Throne and the moment are so solemn and awesome that heaven and earth have to flee away from Him!

What we are going to say now will shock many: Jesus won't be the only Judge at the Bema!

---

[98] John 5:22.

"Don't you know that the saints will judge the world? And if the world is judged by you, are you unworthy to judge the smallest matter?"

"Don't you know that we will judge angels? How much more, things that pertain to this life?"[99]

The above Scriptures state in unequivocal terms that those who will have been saved by believing in Jesus will also participate with Him in pronouncing judgment – not only over the world, but over angels, too!

Not any angel, of course, but angels who followed Lucifer in his rebellion against God[100] and *"Angels who didn't keep their first*

---

[99] 1 Corinthians 6:2-3.
[100] Isaiah 14:11-15. Ezekiel 28:12-17. Revelation 12:3-4.

domain, but deserted their own dwelling place, [whom] *he has kept in everlasting bonds under darkness for the judgment of the great day*"[101].

We know who were the angels who followed Lucifer in his rebellion against God. But who are those angels *"who deserted their own dwelling place"*?

The Nephilim:

The answer to this question is found in the Old Testament. God there unveils this mystery:

---
[101] Jude 6.

"It happened, when men began to multiply on the surface of the ground, and daughters were born to them,

that God's sons saw that men's daughters were beautiful, and they took for themselves wives of all that they chose.

Yahweh said, "My spirit will not strive with man forever, because he also is flesh; yet will his days be one hundred twenty years."

The Nephilim were in the earth in those days, and also after that, when God's sons came to men's daughters. They bore children to them: the same were the mighty men who were of old, men of renown."[102]

God created angels to be at His service in Heaven and to serve a ministry in favour of those who will inherit salvation.[103] For millennia and millennia, they faithfully

---

[102] Genesis 6:1-4.
[103] Hebrews 1:14.

served Him until, one day, their attention was drawn elsewhere.

Men and women had begun to produce beautiful girls. These lovely creatures attracted the attention of some the angels – quite possibly while the latter were on mission on earth.

Eventually, the womanizing angels had sexual relation with human beauties. The product of this weird relationship became a hybrid race called *Nephilim*.

The *Nephilim* grew into giants who became very well-known in the ancient world for their bizarre appearances and superhuman capabilities.

These beings may well have been the giants and heroes whose feats have been narrated by Greco-Roman authors and/or who may have got into certain cultures as gods and semi-gods.

These angels who copulated with humans are those that will be judged by Jesus and believers at the Great White Throne!

We can imagine Jesus as the Supreme Judge and us, believers, as His assessors.

That shows clearly to what status Jesus elevates us when we come to Him! No wonder, we become a new creation!

That's why the apostle Paul reprimanded the Corinthian believers. There were such dissensions among them that sometimes led to litigation in courts of law.[104] In courts of law, they would be judged by unbelievers – which was unbecoming of children of God. Instead, they could bring their grievances before the church authorities who would base

---

[104] 1 Corinthians 6:1.

their judgment on God's Word and not on laws written by unholy and impious people!

Paul's admonition to the Corinthian believers applies to the modern Church, as well. It's a lesson we should learn and practise.

Indeed, there have been cases where one believer has taken a fellow believer to court. Believers have sued pastors, and pastors have sued believers. Worse still, pastors have taken other pastors to court.

Believers – pastors and church members alike – have now found a new "court" where they expose their grievances against one another and try to seek redress. That "court" is … social media!

Allow me to open a parenthesis here to relate an event that illustrates what I've just said.

Recently, there was a case in my own country, which was very shameful. A pastor with about a 40-year career in ministry had an issue with another pastor of the same denomination over the finances of the organization. Instead of settling the matter inwardly, the "aggrieved" pastor took the matter to Facebook and, brandishing papers as evidence, began to publicly expose certain malpractices within the organization!

And that pastor has always been very active in deliverance!

A number of factors made that move even more dramatic and unfortunate. Firstly, although no names were mentioned and Mauritius being a small country, the innuendoes were clear enough to direct the attention of the Christian community to the person(s) being targeted!

Secondly, the Mauritian society is multiracial. There is a high concentration of Hindus who are adamantly anti-Christian. It's already very difficult to bring them to the Lord. Such ill-inspired actions - as that pastor's - don't help to make things any easier – especially as the "victimized" pastor is of Hindu origin! That makes Hindus question the validity of the conversion of those of their kind to Christianity.

Thirdly, the predominantly Hindu government may find in the maladroit act of that pastor reasons to impose certain restrictions upon the Church, thus hindering - and even halting -outreach to Hindus.

That unethical move by that pastor was, definitely, not the best way to settle the contention.

The modern Church would do well to follow Paul's reprimand addressed to the believers in Corinth!

End of parenthesis.

Then all the dead – rich and poor, great and small, white and black, red and yellow, capitalist and communist – find themselves standing before the Throne.

Death and Hades throw up the dead they held captive so that these, too, may stand judgment.

This confirms what we said above – namely that non-believers who die still go to Hades.

You may wonder what about believers at death.

Well, in volume 5, we studied lengthily the subject of the Rapture – the sudden and miraculous catching away of believers - dead and living - by Jesus before the tribulation.[105] At the Rapture, we are judged at the *Bema* to

---

[105] Augustin, Jean Norbert: *Revelation Revisited* Volume 5.

receive - or not - our rewards, as we have explained in chapter 3.

Let's now concentrate on what takes place at the Great White Throne.

Even the sea gives up the dead that were in it for they have to stand judgment, too.

Throughout human history, a number of people have perished at sea and in the sea through suicides, shipwrecks, plane crashes and naval battles. Thousands – if not, millions – of bodies have never been found. But, on that day of retribution, they will all be raised to stand judgment before the Great White Throne!

Just think – as an example - of the 1,500 or so souls who perished when the *Titanic* sank![106]

Of course, I'm not inferring that all the *Titanic* passengers who drowned will be judged at the Great White Throne: I'm sure there were believers among them. But I'm citing this number just to give an idea of the number of people who died in the sea in just one shipwreck!

Just imagine – if you will - the number of people who have died in all the shipwrecks that have happened down through the centuries!

---

[106] Britannica, The Editors of Encyclopaedia. https://www.britannica.com/question/"How many people died when the Titanic sank?". Encyclopedia Britannica, 17 Jul. 2019. Accessed 12 May 2024.

People who died in fires, those who were lost in forests or jungles, those who have been abducted and murdered in unknown places will all be there at the Great White Throne if they never confessed Jesus as their Saviour and Lord.

Those who have perished in floods, earthquakes, wars and epidemics – if unconverted – will rise to face judgment!

If we consider how many people have died since humans have been walking the face of the earth, we'll get an idea of the massive crowd that will be standing at the Great White Throne!

Books will be opened. These are all the records God has kept of people's works, acts, words, thoughts, intentions, motives and so on.

These will be weighed in a balance, as it were, and assessed. Of course, this is just a word picture. Jesus being Divine, He is omniscient and doesn't need a literal balance to know everything about us.

Then there is another book that will be opened: the Book of Life!

This Book is of paramount importance.

In it, is written the name of each and every person who ever accepted Jesus as his or her Saviour and Lord:

*"He who overcomes will be arrayed like this in white garments, and **I will in no way blot***

his name out of the book of life*, and I will confess his name before my Father, and before his angels."*[107]

Once the individual's works will have been examined in the other books, the Book of Life will be used to counter-check. If his or her name is not found written therein, he or she will be cast into the eternal Lake of Fire – no matter how good his or her works will have been! For salvation is found in Jesus Christ only:

"There is salvation in none other, for neither is there any other name under heaven, that is

---

[107] Revelation 3:5, emphasis added.

given among men, in which we must be saved!"[108]

Anyway, the very fact that the individual finds himself or herself standing before the Great White Throne is proof that he or she won't pass the test and will spend eternity in the Lake of Fire.

By examining their works before sending them to their fateful eternal destiny, Jesus will be showing them how futile and worthless their "good" works will have been and how it would have been much easier and more beneficial to accept His sacrifice on the Cross!

---

[108] Acts 4:12.

*"But we are all as an unclean thing, and **all our righteousnesses** (sic) **are as filthy rags;** and we all do fade as a leaf; and our iniquities, like the wind, have taken us away."*[109]

Indeed, in comparison with the blood of Jesus, our works – no matter how good – are but filthy rags. There is no good work that we can perform that could match His blood in efficacy!

Once everyone's works have been checked in the books and counter-checked in the Book of Life, they are thrown into the Lake of Fire.

---

[109] Isaiah 64:6, KJV, emphasis added.

Death and Hades are then cast into the Lake of Fire, too. The Lake of Fire is what is called the second death.

After the "first" death – the separation of soul and body – the wicked are raised to stand trial. But, once thrown into the Lake of Fire, the individual experiences the second death which is definitive and lasts throughout eternity.

"But for the cowardly, unbelieving, sinners, abominable, murderers, sexually immoral, sorcerers, idolaters, and all liars, their part is in the lake that burns with fire and sulfur, which is the second death."[110]

---

[110] Revelation 21:8.

No wonder the Scriptures tell us that

"The last enemy that shall be destroyed is death."[111]

Thus will end human history on this earth.

---

[111] 1 Corinthians 15:26., KJV.

CONCLUSION

With everything that's happening in the world – the Covid-19, global warming, flooding in almost all the continents, drought in other places, war in Ukraine, war between Israel and Hamas, transgenderism even in "Christian" circles, rampant antisemitism and so many other things, people everywhere are saying things like "It's the end times. We are living in the end times. The world is moving to its end" …

Believers and non-believers alike are conscious that the end is coming.

Sadly and tragically, though, there are many who are careless, skeptical and rebellious who, instead, see the world developing even more! With the advent of Artificial Intelligence (AI), their hope for an ever better world has grown sky-high. Atheists feel comforted in their belief that God is but a fallacy. We are seeing a resurgence of humanism in its worst form.

Even the Church is dangerously slipping towards the lukewarm state that Jesus found in the church in Laodicea.[112] False doctrines and all sorts of spirits have been allowed to creep in. Sin among clergy and laity is rampant. The prosperity gospel is appealing

---

[112] Revelation 3:14-22.

to greater and greater numbers and has supplanted the true Gospel of grace.

Yet, the resurrected Jesus has made known to us through His servant John *"the things which must happen soon"*.[113]

Thus, in this volume, we have examined essentially the very last events that will take place in this world's final days.

We have looked at the battle of Gog and Magog, the question of death, the afterlife, Jesus's ministry to the dead in Sheol, the judgment of the just at the Bema, the

---

[113] Revelation 1:1.

judgment of the wicked at the Great White Throne and the second death.

"All the world's a stage
And all the men and women merely players;
They have their exits and their entrances"[114].

These few lines written by the great English playwright, William Shakespeare, aptly summarizes man's passage in this world. The world is compared to a theatre with its stage. Men and women – the actors and actresses – appear from behind the curtain, play their part and disappear behind the curtain. Some are heroes and heroines; others are villains.

---
[114] William Shakespeare: *As You Like It.*

Likewise, God created the world, thus setting the stage. Then He created the man Adam who was supposed to be the main male character. Next, He created the first woman, Eve, who was to be the main female character.

As time passed, the villain appeared on the world scene – the devil, the Serpent of old, the dragon: Satan!

But hero and heroine were, unfortunately, deceived and vanquished by the villain.

From then on, unfortunately, the villain took things into his own hands and became the main character. Gathering a host of acolytes around him, he lorded it over the world scene. This went on until …

Well, until the Supreme Director decided to send from backstage another Hero – the Hero of heroes – to put an end to the villain's tyranny!

From then on, the days of the villain were numbered.

Realizing that the villain was no match for Him, the Hero of heroes allowed the villain to have his own way to see how far he'll go in his despotism.

Then when the villain crossed the red line and the cup was full to the brim, the Hero of heroes confronted him in an epic battle on a battle field called Calvary!

That was where the villain and his acolytes were utterly defeated, the Hero of heroes thus demonstrating His supremacy over them:

"he has taken it out that way, nailing it to the cross; having stripped the principalities and the powers, he made a show of them openly, triumphing over them in it."[115]

With the villain's defeat, the play came to an end as in every good movie.

All that was left now was for the Supreme Director-Producer to remunerate the actors and actresses according to their performance in the play.

---

[115] Colossians 2:14-15.

Those who played their part well and sided with the Hero of heroes, receive a fabulous reward in the Latter's Eternal Abode.

But those who, alas, chose to join the ranks of the villain ... well, they go to eternal damnation!

Yet,

"... God so loved the world, that he gave his one and only Son, that whoever believes in him should not perish, but have eternal life."[116]

---

[116] John 3:16.

Milton Keynes UK
Ingram Content Group UK Ltd.
UKHW012130110624
443988UK00001B/67